I·N·C·R·E·D·I·B·L·E
ANIMALS
A TO Z

FROM THE PUBLISHERS OF
RANGER RICK MAGAZINE

NATIONAL WILDLIFE FEDERATION

National Wildlife Federation

Copyright © 1985 National Wildlife Federation.
All rights reserved. Reproduction of the
whole or any part of the contents without
written permission is prohibited.

Library of Congress CIP Data: page 95

INTRODUCTION

INCREDIBLE ANIMALS A TO Z whisks you off on a global tour to see some of the world's most bizarre animals. You will stop in Australia to see a lizard that gets its drinking water by collecting dew on its scales; and in Africa you will find a giant monkey that growls and snarls when it is happy—and yawns when it is angry. But for all that we can tell you about these fantastic creatures, there are mysteries, too. We don't know why some stag beetles have such large jaws, or why the emperor tamarin monkey has such a long mustache. Maybe someday you will be the one to uncover the answers.

Giant Anteater

A

ANTEATERS

It's hard to believe that some large animals can live on just ants and termites. But the creatures called anteaters do very well on this diet.

The six-foot-long *giant anteater* (left) is the largest member of an anteater family that lives in Central and South America. With strong claws, it tears open the insects' nests. Then it pulls out its food with its sticky, two-foot-long tongue. Female anteaters like this one often carry their young while hunting. The mothers feed their babies milk until the youngsters are old enough to find their own ants and termites to eat.

The *lesser anteater* (bottom right) has the same diet as the giant anteater, but doesn't grow as big. When it feels threatened, the lesser anteater stands up and strikes out at its enemies. The *silky anteater* (bottom left) is the smallest member of the family. Its name refers to its silky fur.

Australia's *spiny anteater* (right above) belongs to an entirely different family. It also uses sharp claws and a sticky tongue to gather ants and termites. When it is in danger, it rolls itself into a ball. Its sharp spines discourage enemies.

Spiny Anteater

Silky Anteater

Lesser Anteater

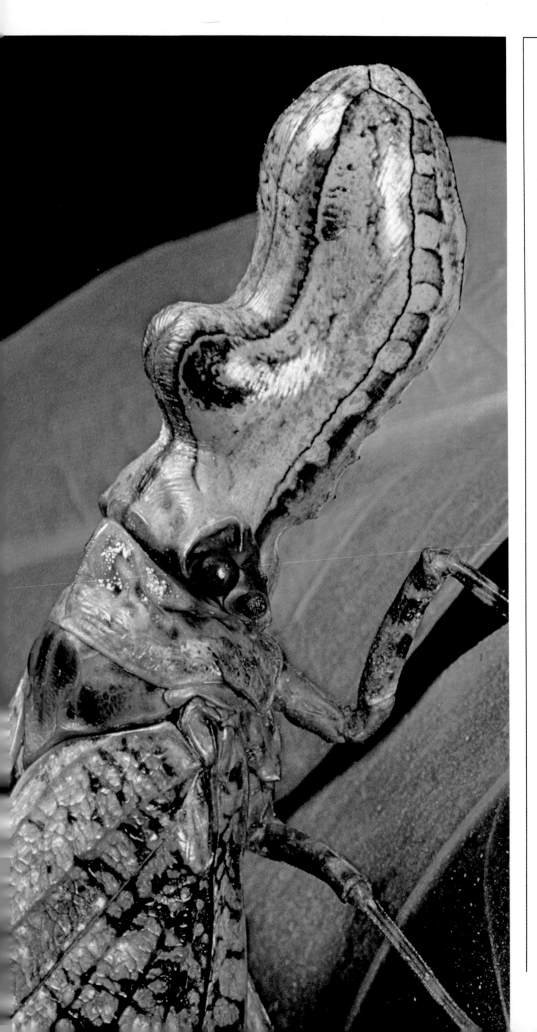

 A

ALLIGATOR BUG

At first glance, the South American alligator bug looks like a tiny, smiling alligator no longer than your hand. But look closer. Those "teeth" are just marks on the bug's head. And so are the giant "eyes." The bug's real eyes are small and lie a bit below and behind the false ones.

This bug lives in the tops of trees, where it is always in danger of being eaten by monkeys and other animals. Scientists think the bug's strange appearance may help keep it safe by scaring away dangerous predators.

ARROW CRAB

Like a pyramid with legs, the arrow crab slowly pokes its way along the ocean floor looking for food. Its eyes are the two balls attached partway up its tall, pointed head. This thin-legged crab is a scavenger. It feeds mainly on tiny scraps of rotting plants and dead fish floating in the water. These scraps get caught on the crab's spiny body, and the crab pulls them off and eats them.

Being hard-shelled and spindly has its advantages. When trying to eat the crabs, fish find that the long legs get in the way. So, they leave the crabs alone. But sometimes two male or two female arrow crabs fight and break off each other's legs. Then fish eat what's left of the loser.

AXOLOTL

Like Peter Pan, the axolotl (AK-suh-lot-ull) is a youngster that never completely grows up. Only this youngster is a six-inch-long salamander. It lives only in lakes near Mexico City, Mexico.

Most salamanders spend the first part of their lives under water in an immature form. They look a lot like the axolotl. They have feathery gills that let them get oxygen from the water. Then, after a few weeks or months, they mature. They lose their gills and start living on land. But the axolotl spends its entire life under water. In fact, its name comes from an Aztec Indian word meaning "water toy."

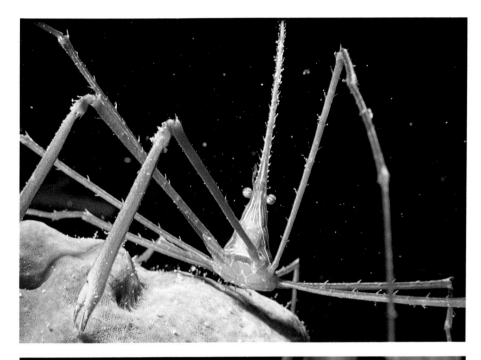

ANGLERFISH

Hundreds of feet below the ocean's surface, the sea is cold and dark. Food is scarce and difficult to see. In this gloomy world, the anglerfish catches its meals with a built-in fishing pole that sticks out from its head. The end of the pole even glows to attract something for dinner.

The anglerfish rests almost motionless in the water. Only the glowing tip of its fishing pole moves, waving back and forth. Scientists are not sure what makes the tip glow. It may hold special bacteria that create their own light. Whatever causes the glow, the moving light attracts curious fish. As a fish swims closer, the anglerfish swings the tip of its pole down, leading its victim right into its mouth.

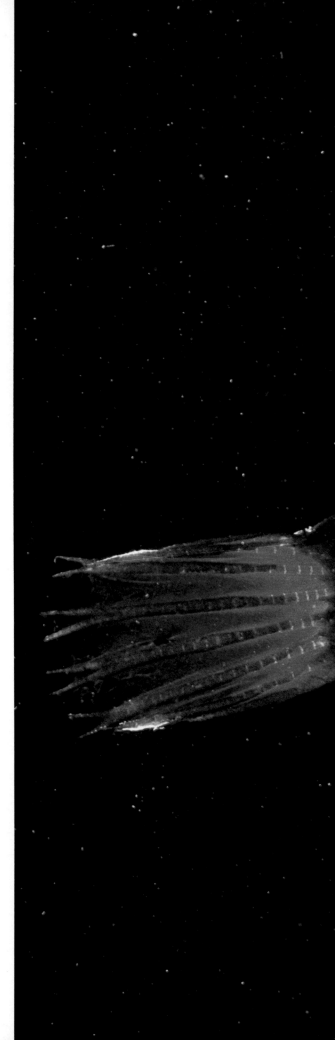

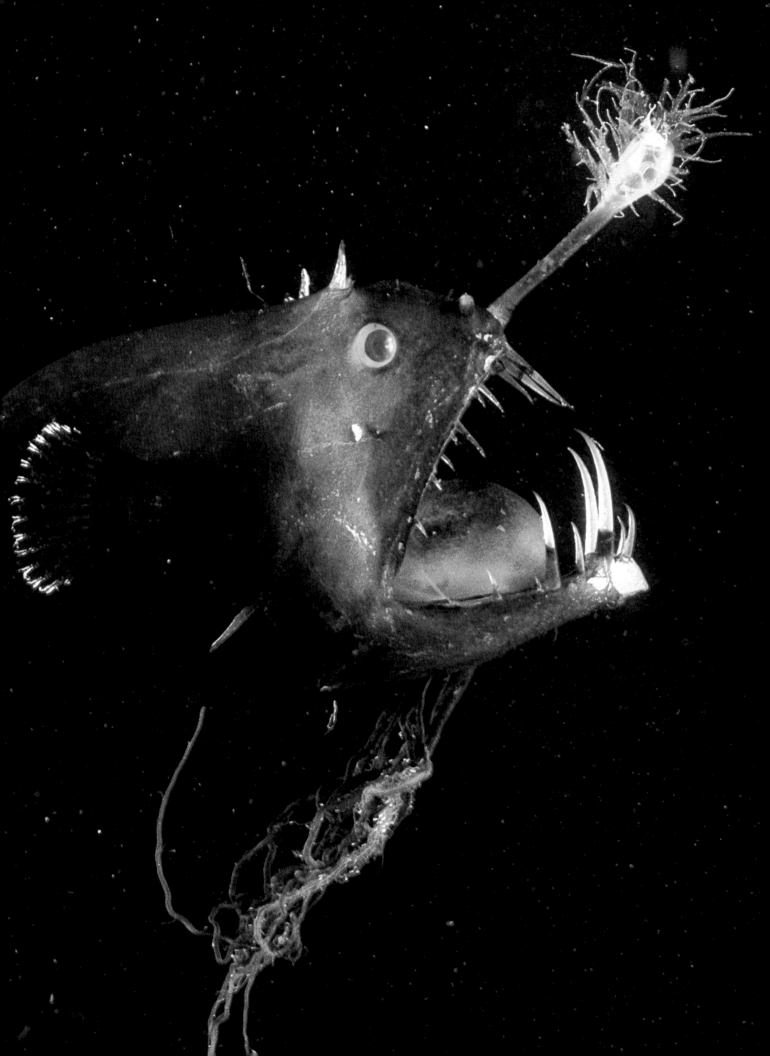

B

BLUE-FOOTED BOOBY

Blue-footed boobies look and act like slow-witted clowns. Sailors named these Latin American birds boobies, which means "dunces," because the birds seemed so stupid. They would sit still as the sailors walked over to them and picked them up.

The blue-footed booby is no dummy when it comes to finding food in the sea. When one bird spots a school of fish, it signals the other boobies by whistling. Then the entire flock dives for dinner.

The booby seen here is dancing to attract a female. If the female is interested, she will join in the dance.

BOMBARDIER BEETLE

The bombardier beetle is strange because it can use chemical warfare against its enemies. Glands inside the beetle's body produce and store chemicals that explode when the beetle mixes them in a special chamber in its body.

The explosion sprays out a hot, smelly liquid. The tiny blast doesn't hurt the beetle, but the spray burns the attacker and scares it away.

If you pick up one of these beetles, you will be sprayed, too. But the amount of liquid is so small it will just feel a bit warm on your skin.

BRITTLE STAR

Toy animals may break, but real animals don't—or do they? Brittle stars, relatives of starfish, reproduce both by laying eggs and by breaking themselves in half. Each half then grows back the missing parts to make a whole, new animal. Scientists once found a small reef covered by brittle stars that they think came from one individual.

Brittle stars may look slow to us, but to their relatives they are speed demons. People walk at about four miles per hour. Brittle stars crawl at two miles per *day*—but that is ten times faster than starfish.

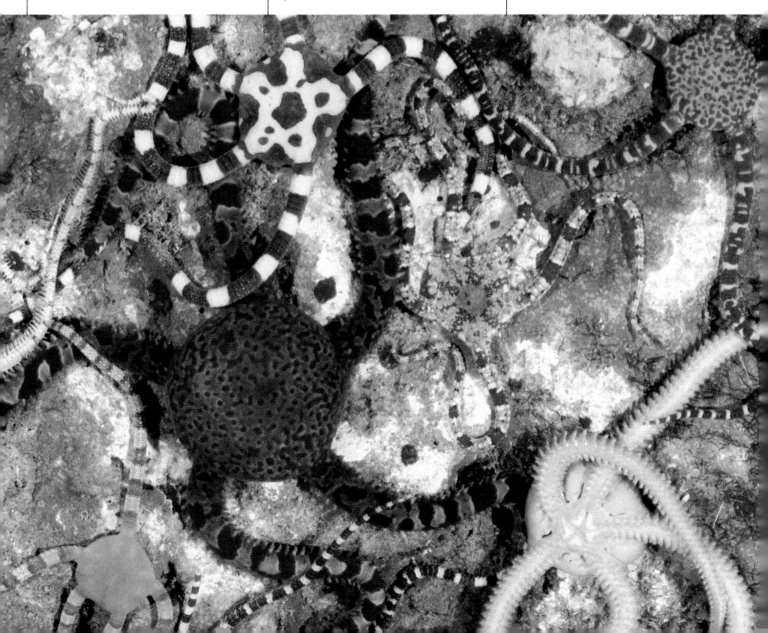

Fishing Bat

Hammerheaded Bat

Pygmy Fruit-eating Bat

Yellow-winged Bat

B

BATS

Bats belong to the same group of animals—mammals—that includes dogs and cats, horses and cows, pandas and people. But bats are the only mammals that can really fly. They take to the sky at night in search of food.

About 70 percent of all bats eat insects. Like the *yellow-winged bat* (bottom), they use sounds to find their prey. They send out squeaks that are too high-pitched for humans to hear. Then their extra-large ears pick up the echoes as they bounce off the prey the bats are chasing.

The *fishing bat* (far left) uses its echoes to find fish. Skimming along the surface of a stream, it sends out squeaks that bounce off the water. A ripple on the water's surface may mean that a fish is near. If the bat detects a ripple, it swings down its claws and, if it's lucky, hauls up dinner.

The *hammerheaded bat* (top) doesn't need sounds to find its food. Its keen sense of smell and good eyesight help it locate the sweet African fruits that make up its diet.

When the *pygmy fruit-eating bat* (center) finishes its meal, it retires to a most un-usual home. It makes its own tent out of palm leaves. The bat bites the leaves so they will bend, creating a snug shelter.

13

CHAMELEON

Almost everything about a chameleon is strange. The 5-inch tongue of this chameleon is as long as its body. It zips out to snag insects.

While the chameleon sits on a branch, its eyes turn in different directions. One eye may look up or down as the other looks forward or back.

Some chameleons can change color to blend in with their surroundings. They do this by changing the size of different colored cells under their skin. Changing color helps chameleons hide from enemies. Chameleons also change colors to tell each other that they are ready to fight or ready to give up.

COCONUT CRAB

Did you ever see a crab climb a tree? On some islands in the Indian and Pacific oceans, coconut crabs climb palm trees with ease. Some people say the crabs climb so they can cut down the coconuts. Others think the crabs are looking for fresh water trapped by the leaves. On the ground, the crabs eat the pulp of the coconuts. Scientists are not sure if the crabs break open the coconuts or just take ones that are already cracked.

CLOWN SHRIMP

It looks like a funny clown in a pink polka-dot suit. But the Hawaiian clown shrimp is a clever hunter. The 2½-inch-long clown shrimp dines on starfish that live on Hawaii's coral reefs. The clown shrimp flips a starfish over onto its back. That exposes the soft flesh underneath. Then, using its powerful claws, the shrimp cuts off the flesh and eats it. Getting the starfish turned over is hard work, but it pays off. The clown shrimp can live for two days on a meal of just one 6-inch starfish.

CAVE CRAYFISH

The blind cave crayfish moves slowly in its underground world. But it does not travel that way because it is lazy or can't find its way. Moving slowly saves energy. The slower it moves, the less food the crayfish needs to eat. And in its world of complete darkness, food is scarce.

Although this ghostly creature is blind, its long antennae help it find prey. The antennae can detect any motion in the water. When the crayfish senses movement—perhaps an insect washed into the cave by a heavy rain—it swims straight out to its prey and nabs it.

CASSOWARY

It runs faster than a racing man and leaps four-foot-high bushes in a single jump. It dashes headfirst through the forest with its head protected by a thick, bony helmet. It swims across rivers and fights with its feet like a karate champion. Indeed, the cassowary could be called "superbird." But this 100-pound native of Australia and New Guinea is really shy. If you came near a cassowary in the forest, it would probably run away. It fights only when it feels cornered. The bird's claws are sharp enough to rip open almost any animal that would attack it. But stories of how the birds chase and kill people are rumors. In fact, more people have probably heard the cassowary's deep booming call than have ever seen the bird.

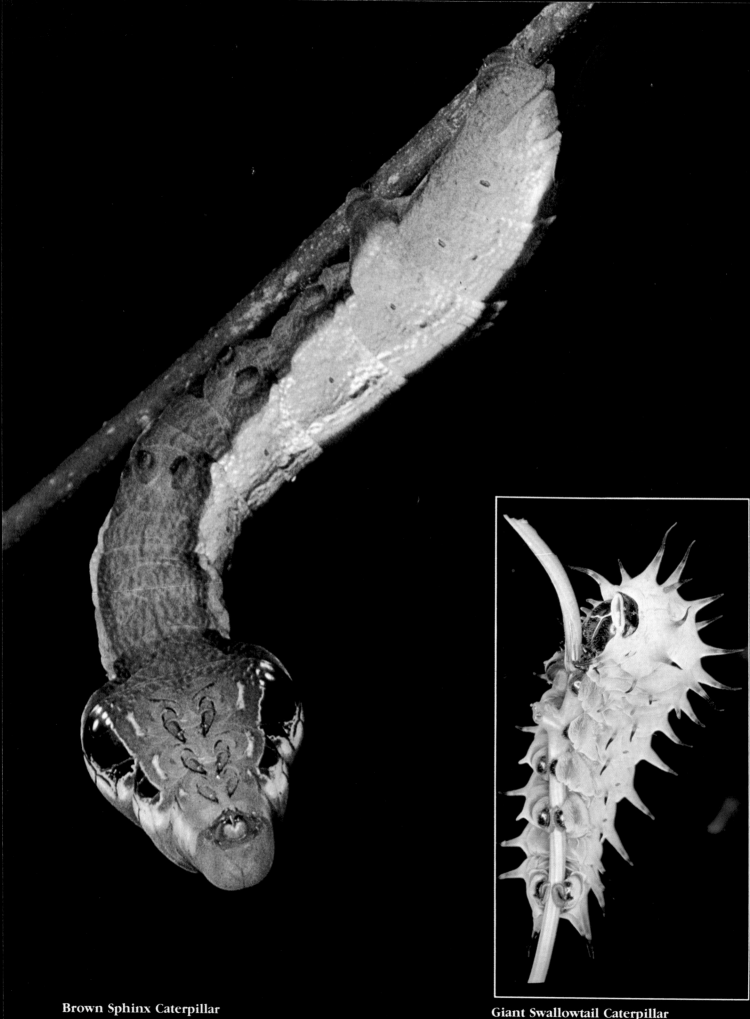

Brown Sphinx Caterpillar
Giant Swallowtail Caterpillar

CATERPILLARS

Caterpillars munching their way through the trees are a common sight. But these creatures have so many enemies it's surprising that any survive to become moths and butterflies. Lizards feast on them. Some flies and wasps lay eggs on them. And birds pick them right off the leaves. Luckily, caterpillars have spines, stingers, and disguises that help protect them.

That's not really a snake on the far left. It's a *brown sphinx caterpillar*. When it puffs out its sides, two spots make the caterpillar look like a snake, scaring away birds.

When danger threatens the *giant swallowtail caterpillar* (left inset), the caterpillar sticks out hidden red horns to frighten its enemies. Horns and a large body also make a harmless *hickory horned devil* (below left) look scary.

The *mourning cloak's* spots (below right) warn enemies that it has tough spines. Furry tentacles make the *monkey slug caterpillar* (bottom right) look like a fuzzy octopus. But its "fur" is really a covering of stinging hairs. The *saddleback* (bottom left) looks like a perfect target. But the "saddle" is a warning to enemies to watch out for its stinging hairs.

Hickory Horned Devil

Mourning Cloak

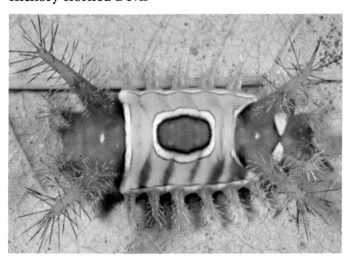

Saddleback Caterpillar

Monkey Slug Caterpillar

D

DRAGONET

The male dragonet fish is all flash. Only a few inches long, it has to be bright to get noticed. The more colorful it is, the better chance it has of standing out from other male dragonets and being chosen by a female as a mate.

Female dragonets are much less colorful. They look so drab by comparison that scientists once thought they were a different kind of fish.

There are more than 50 species of dragonets. All live near the ocean's floor. Most stay in the shallow parts of mild waters around the world. But the dragonet fish seen here lives nearly a mile down in the Pacific Ocean near the Philippine Islands.

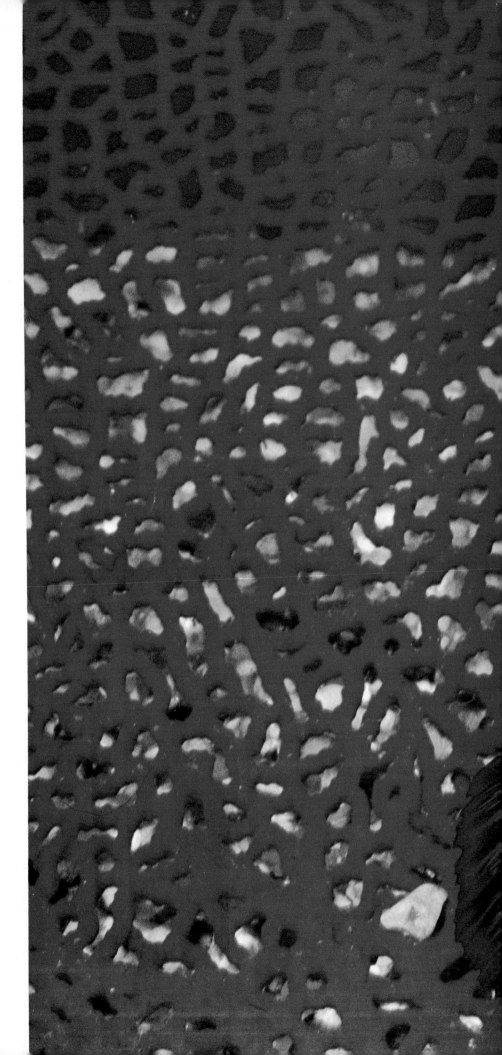

E

ELEPHANT SHREW

Elephant shrews aren't shrews at all. And they obviously aren't elephants, either. These furry African animals are just a foot long. They got their name from their long noses, which do look a little like elephant trunks. These noses are good for poking through leaves in search of food. Elephant shrews eat ants, termites, and other insects.

Some elephant shrews sound like crickets when they call each other. When they are scared, some thump their hind feet on the ground. Others sound an alarm by beating the ground with their tails.

EMPEROR TAMARIN

Its long, white mustache makes the emperor tamarin monkey look like an old-fashioned king or emperor. The mustache doesn't seem to serve any real purpose. At least scientists have not found one. But if its mustache gets dirty, an emperor tamarin tries very hard to clean it.

Emperor tamarins, which live in the forests of Brazil and Peru and eat fruit and insects, were not discovered until 1907. They are so rare they are not seen in zoos very often.

ELEPHANT SEAL

It may look like a floppy, four-ton sausage, but a bull elephant seal rules the beach when it comes ashore. It's easy to see how this funny-looking creature got its name. It is a seal, all right, an air-breathing mammal that lives in the water. But it's also very heavy. It is as long as a car and weighs almost as much as an elephant. And its snout sticks out like an elephant's trunk.

In breeding season, the bulls fight over the females. They roar and bite each other. Their long, droopy noses swell up, and probably act as echo chambers to make the roaring even louder. A noisy bull can be heard miles away. The winning bull gets to keep a harem of 30 to 40 female seals.

ELECTRIC CATFISH

Like other catfish and four-legged cats, the electric catfish has long, sensitive whiskers. Catfish use these whiskers to probe for food in the bottoms of streams. But this African fish also uses something that's even more unusual: electricity. The fish sends out a weak electric current into the muddy water where it cannot see. Other fish swimming close by interrupt the electric current. The catfish can feel the change. It then knows that a meal is at hand.

This catfish can also send out an electric current strong enough to light up three 100-watt bulbs. Some people think the catfish does this to shock other fish. They say the shock makes a fish lose its dinner. Then the catfish could gobble down the food the other fish threw up.

Ancient Egyptians used the catfish to give shocks to sick people. They thought the shocks would help cure them. Egyptians called the fish "he who releases many" because fishermen who were shocked would drop their catch.

F

FRIGATE BIRD

The bright red throat sac tells us that this male frigate bird is either guarding his nest or showing off. The bright color attracts females. It also warns other males to stay away. The male keeps his red signal inflated until his mate lays her first egg.

Though the frigate bird lives by the sea, its feathers are not waterproof. It cannot land on the water as some other fish-eating birds do. Instead, it dives at other birds in the air to make them drop their catch. Then it snags the dropped food in midair.

FRILLED LIZARD

Does this Australian frilled lizard scare you? It's certainly trying to. That's how this harmless creature defends itself. If some other animal threatens it, the lizard first runs away. Then it suddenly stops, spins around, and fans out its wide frill, a flap of skin that normally lies flat against its sides. At the same time, it hisses angrily.

F

FLASHLIGHT FISH

Now you see it; now you don't. That's the flashlight fish of the Red Sea turning its glowing lights on and off. These three-inch-long fish swim in small groups just a few feet below the surface. They are looking for worms and other small creatures to eat. The blinking lights attract their prey—and confuse their enemies. When a predator gets too close, the flashlight fish, like the one in the small photograph, shuts off its light and swims away. The sudden disappearance of the light startles the predator and gives the fish time to escape.

These fish don't really make their own light. Billions of bacteria grow in a special organ just below each eye. These bacteria glow and create the light. The fish turns off the light by raising a fold of skin like an upside-down eyelid to cover the glowing organ.

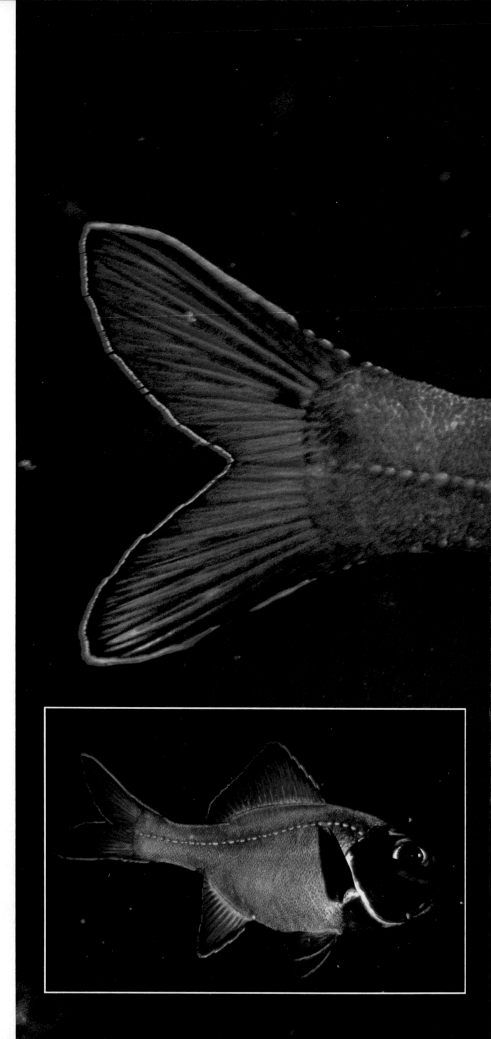

F

FROGS

The frog family includes acrobats, fighters, and some of the deadliest animals on earth.

Like its many tree-climbing relatives, the *red-eyed tree frog* (this page) can climb even tiny branches. Extra-wide toes help it get a better grip.

The *arrow-poison frog* (top of next page) is as dangerous as its name suggests. Indians in South America take poison from its skin to coat the arrows they use when hunting. A single ounce from one type of arrow-poison frog is enough to kill 100,000 animals.

Its large snout makes the *spatulate-nosed frog* easy to identify (top right). When the weather is too hot and dry, it crawls into a hole and plugs up the entrance with its nose.

Dull colors and pointed flaps of skin make the *Asian horned frog* (bottom right) look like the leaves it sits on. This frog also has tough spades on its feet for digging out a home in the dirt.

The *South African bullfrog* (bottom left) doesn't look like it's afraid of anything. And it probably isn't. It puffs itself up and turns on its enemies as a way of saying, "Go away!"

The female *marsupial frog* (top left) carries her eggs in a pouch on her back. When the eggs are ready to hatch, she opens the pouch with her toes.

Red-eyed Tree Frog

Arrow-poison Frog

Marsupial Frog

Spatulate-nosed Frog

South African Bullfrog

Asian Horned Frog

29

G

GOOSEFISH

One person called it "the ugliest fish I've ever seen." And looking at it, it's hard to imagine any kind of animal uglier than the goosefish. This nearly flat creature is as long as many people are tall—about five feet. And it weighs more than fifty pounds.

Like the anglerfish on pages 8 and 9, the goosefish attracts prey with a built-in "fishing bait." The bait is a thin piece of skin that waves back and forth just above the fish's huge mouth. When another fish comes close to check out the bait, the goosefish swallows the other fish in one gulp.

Sometimes the goosefish tries to eat fish that are almost as big as it is. When swimming near the surface, it will even eat ducks and other sea birds—maybe even geese.

There are several kinds of goosefish around the world. This one is the American goosefish. It lives in the Atlantic Ocean from Nova Scotia south to the Carolinas.

G

GLASSWING

Butterflies are known for their bright, colorful wings. But the wings of the glasswing butterfly of Panama have no color at all. You can see right through them. Hiding is no problem for this creature. All it has to do is sit still and let the leaves behind it show through.

Different clear-winged butterflies have different ways of letting the light pass through their wings. Some have wings without any scales. Others, like the glasswing below, have wings with scales that look like fine hair. The hairs are so thin they do not block the light.

The bright, white spots on the wings of this butterfly are not reflections. They are really larger scales that are white. As the glasswing moves its wings, the spots seem to flash on and off. The flashes divert a predator's attention away from the butterfly's body. If a bird attacks the spot, all it gets is a mouthful of tough wing. Very often the glasswing can break loose and get away.

GECKO

The gecko has been called the world's only talking reptile. The trouble is, it knows only one word: "Gecko!" At least, that's the sound one type of gecko makes. And that sound has given all these lizards their name.

There are many different kinds of gecko. One may be the world's smallest reptile. It was found on an island in the Caribbean and measured less than 1½ inches long.

People who have a gecko in the house may be surprised to see it run up the wall and hang upside down from the ceiling. The animal's feet are covered with millions of tiny, hooked hairs. These hairs can hold the gecko onto almost any surface, even glass.

H

HONEY ANTS

Can you imagine eating until you are ready to burst? Some honey ants do just that. When food is plentiful, ant workers gather nectar from flowers and take it underground to special ants called honeypots, or repletes (ri-PLEETS). Soon the repletes fill up with nectar until they are the size of small grapes. When the outside food supplies are gone, the workers get food a special way. They rub the repletes, which then spit out a fresh meal of nectar.

Native Americans used to dig up the repletes and use them as food.

H

HORNBILL

If you're ever in the middle of an Asian jungle and hear a train coming, don't worry. It's not a locomotive on the loose. It is only noisy hornbills flying by. These turkey-sized birds make really strange, loud sounds when they flap their wings. The birds look strange, too. They have double-decker beaks and long, dark eye-lashes. Even their family life is odd. When the female is ready to lay her eggs, the male seals her into a hollow tree. She helps by plugging up the opening from the inside. Only a small hole is left where the male can pass food to his mate. She sheds her feathers and stays inside the tree caring for the young for three months or more. When her feathers finally grow back, she chips her way out and flies off to help gather food for the growing family.

H

HAMMERHEAD SHARK

The strange shape of the hammerhead shark is a big mystery. The animal's eyes and nostrils are stuck out on the ends of a wide "hammer" head. On the largest sharks, about 20 feet long, this head can be a yard wide. No one is sure why the shark's head is shaped this way. It may help the shark keep its balance when swimming fast. Or having nostrils so far apart may help the shark locate prey better by smell. After all, hav-ing an ear on each side of the head helps humans tell what directions sounds come from.

A hungry hammerhead has no trouble gulping down other fish, even smaller sharks and poisonous stingrays. These sharks rarely attack humans, but they can be dangerous.

HATCHETFISH

They look like monsters in a nightmare. But they are only hatchetfish prowling the ocean nearly 1,500 feet below the surface. Their eyes are so sensitive the fish would be blinded by daylight. But at night, the fish do come closer to the surface in search of food. They eat microscopic animals and the young of other fish. The hatchetfish's eyes may act as magnifiers, making such small prey easier to find.

Hatchetfish "monsters" are much too small to be danger-ous to people. Each adult is just a little more than one inch long. And it takes about 500 of them to weigh one pound.

I

ICHNEUMON WASP

This female ichneumon (ick-NEW-muhn) wasp looks like she is stinging a tree. But what's *really* happening is even more odd. She is laying her eggs inside the tree. Here's how she does it.

She lands on a tree where larvae of other insects are living beneath the bark. Then she pushes her long egg depositor through the bark and lays an egg in or next to the larva, called a host.

After the egg hatches, the baby ichneumon feeds on the larva host. It stays under the bark all summer. When winter comes, it spins a cocoon. In the spring, it comes out of the cocoon as an adult wasp and chews its way out of the tree.

IGUANA

The only lizards in the world that feed in the sea live on the Galapagos Islands in the Pacific Ocean. These are the marine iguana (ih-GWAN-uh) lizards. They are more than four feet long, and they are found nowhere else on earth. They swim and dive down to nibble on seaweed.

Marine iguanas can even drink salt water. Special glands on their snouts get rid of the excess salt.

IMPEYAN PHEASANT

"Hey, look at me!" That's the signal the male impeyan (im-PAY-un) pheasant sends to females with its bright colors. To a hungry eagle, the signal also says "Come and get it!" But don't be fooled. This Asian mountain pheasant keeps a ready eye out for danger. In a flash it can head for cover.

When cold weather comes, some birds migrate long distances to the south. The impeyan pheasant has it much easier. It just flies downhill into the warmer valleys. When warm weather returns, it goes back up into the mountains.

In any season, this bird is well equipped to dig out its meals of roots and grubs. Its tough beak makes a good shovel. In no time it can dig a hole a foot deep.

ICEFISH

A fish without any blood? That's what seamen thought when they caught their first icefish. As it turns out, icefish do have blood. Their blood is colorless, though, because it has no red cells. Most fish and other animals need red blood cells to carry oxygen from their gills or lungs to the rest of their bodies. Oxygen enables the animals to turn their food into energy. Icefish move so slowly they don't need much energy. So they don't need much oxygen and don't have any red blood cells at all.

People call the fish *icefish* because they are milky white like the ice in Antarctic waters where the fish live.

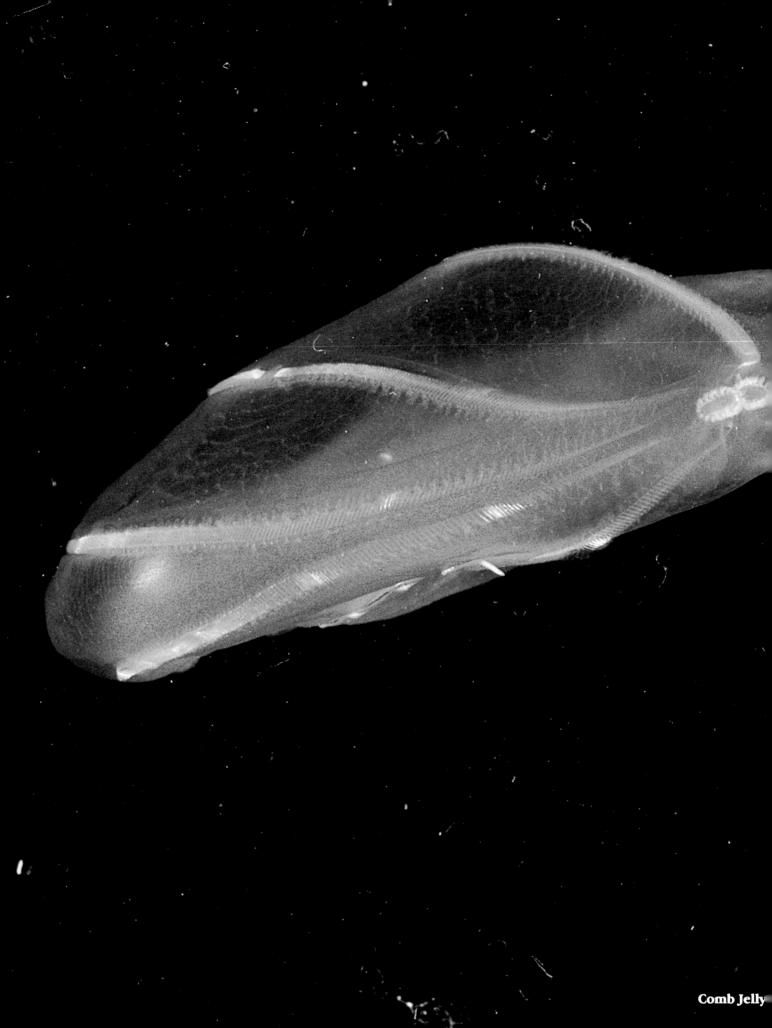

Comb Jelly

Mastigias Jellyfish

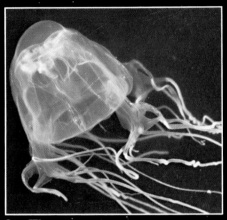

Sea Wasp

Extended Jellyfish

Formosa Jellyfish

JELLYFISH

Jellyfish don't look like animals at all. They are some of the strangest creatures in the ocean. Large white lumps make the *Mastigias jellyfish* (top photo) and the *extended jellyfish* (third from top) look like floating cauliflower. The white lumps are covered with thousands of tiny mouths. As the jellyfish swim, these mouths take in food almost too small to see.

The *Formosa jellyfish* (bottom photo) and the *sea wasp* (second from top) wave long tentacles covered with stinging poison cells. These cells are deadly enough to kill fish and other creatures that touch them. For swimmers off the coast of Australia, sea wasps are more dangerous than sharks.

Even on the beach a jelly-fish can be harmful. Its tenta-cles still sting if they are touched. But a jellyfish stranded on the sand soon dries up and disappears.

The *comb jelly* (far left) is a different kind of jellyfish. It has no branches or stinging cells. It looks more like a clear fly-ing saucer. Its pale colors come from nearly a million tiny hairs running in rows from front to back. These hairs beat together and drive the creature mouth-first through the sea.

KING VULTURE

Vultures live on dead, rotting animals. So, it's a good thing they can't smell what they eat. But the king vulture is different. It eats carrion, but it also attacks live animals. And it can smell. It is one of the very few birds in the world that has a sense of smell.

People in Latin America have watched king vultures search for meals. These birds go right to dead animals, even ones hidden in the thick underbrush of the dark forest. They have to be able to smell food to find it in such dark places. The orange balls of fat hanging over the top of the vultures' beaks may help the birds to detect odors. So far, however, scientists have not learned for sure what the fatty balls are for.

KATYDID

"Katy did! Katy didn't!" That's the mating call that gives the katydid its name. On a late summer night, the air is filled with these insects' loud sounds. But don't look in your backyard for this strange-looking katydid. It lives in South America. If you ever see one, be careful. Its strong jaws can give a bad bite.

There are about 5,000 kinds of katydids around the world. Each kind makes a different sound. Experts can tell one kind of katydid from another just by listening.

Like their relatives the crickets, katydids sing by rubbing their wings together. It's a little bit like rubbing your thumbnail across the teeth of a comb: One of a katydid's wings scrapes across tiny ridges on the other wing.

For most kinds of katydids, it's the male that makes all the noise. Some females answer, but only with a soft ticking sound. Most female katydids can't make any sounds at all. So it's up to them to find the singing male.

K

KIWI

They can't fly. They don't have tails. Their wings are almost hidden under their feathers. And their feathers look a lot like hair. So, it's hard to believe that the little brown kiwis of New Zealand are really birds. But they are birds, about the size of chickens. And they lay the largest eggs—compared with the size of the female—of any birds on earth. An 8-pound hen may lay a 1-pound egg.

Once the eggs are laid, the males take over. They sit on the eggs and guard them for nearly three months. After the chicks hatch, the males lead them through the forest to look for worms and insects.

LEAFY SEA DRAGON

This curious critter looks like a cross between a horse and a lettuce salad. But it is really a fish, Australia's leafy sea dragon. The spines and leafy flaps of skin that stick out in all directions help the foot-long fish hide among the plants on the bottom of the sea, where it feeds. The sea dragon's snout sucks in worms and other small creatures.

When it's time to raise young sea dragons, the father does most of the work. The fertilized eggs stick to his body. He carries them around for a few weeks until they hatch and the young grow large enough to swim away.

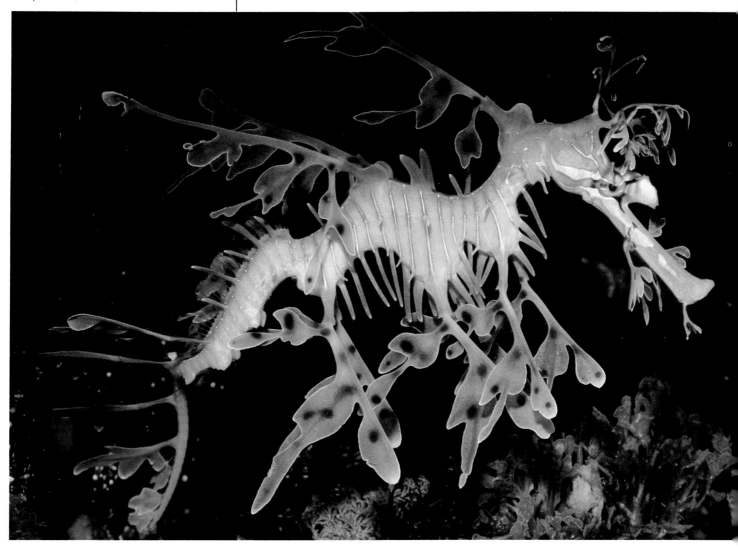

LUNA MOTH

Adult luna moths are big, but they have short lives. They live for barely two weeks. In that brief time, they must find mates and lay eggs.

To attract males, the females give off a special smell. The males use their sensitive antennae to detect that smell. Once they mate and lay eggs, the adults die. Their young hatch as caterpillars in the summer. The caterpillars spend the winter wrapped tightly in cocoons on the ground. When warm weather arrives, they come out as beautiful, green, adult moths.

LIONFISH

Look, but don't touch! Skin divers in the Pacific and Indian oceans know to stay away from the beautiful lionfish. Its long, colorful spines carry poison glands as dangerous as those of a poisonous snake. Touching the spines may not kill you, but the sting hurts.

If the lionfish thinks it is in danger, it attacks. It uses its poisonous spines to poke and jab at whatever threatens it—even a skin diver.

The lionfish doesn't always have to use its spines for protection. Its colors warn others that it is not good to eat.

LAMPREY

Lampreys are living proof that it is not always necessary to have jaws to eat meat. Adult lampreys don't have jaws. They clamp onto the side of a fish with their round mouths. Then their spine-covered tongues scrape off pieces of flesh. At one time, the Great Lakes had so many lampreys they were killing off large numbers of fish. Now the lampreys are under control.

All lampreys are born blind and look like tiny worms. They spend six or seven years buried at the bottom of streams before turning into adults.

MORAY EELS

Moray eels look like big underwater snakes with small heads and sharp teeth. In fact, they are fish. But they are unusual ones. Most fish have scales and two or more fins. Morays are scaleless. They have one long fin that runs like a ribbon down their backs, around their tails, and part way up their stomachs. Their bodies, four to five feet long, are covered by slime.

Morays are fierce fighters. They attack and eat fish and other small creatures that live near coral reefs and rocky shores in warm waters. Because of their shape, they move easily among the coral and rocks on the ocean floor. They chase their prey into small places and grab them with daggerlike teeth.

The *green moray* (top photo) looks like it's about to catch a meal. But most likely it's just breathing. To breathe, morays constantly open and close their mouths. That way they force water over their gills and take in oxygen. Because of the way they breathe, morays must eat their food whole. They can't bite off pieces and chew because if they closed their mouths, they would suffocate.

Morays cannot see very well. But they do have a keen sense of smell that helps them find their prey. They smell through tubelike nostrils. The *ribbon moray* (bottom photo) has nostrils that spread out at the ends. The eel waits, coiled in a narrow opening, and darts out like a snake when it smells a meal nearby.

The *slender moray* (middle photo), like most morays, looks drab and dull. But some morays, like the *dragon moray* (opposite page), are colorful. Spots help this eel hide by blending into the bright reefs where it lives.

A moray eel's bite can be very painful, but you'd be in bigger trouble if you bit a moray. These eels live on smaller fish that sometimes eat poisonous plants. The poison doesn't hurt the morays, but it does make its way into their flesh. Then the eels themselves become poisonous. Anyone eating them could become sick and perhaps die.

Green Moray

Slender Moray

Ribbon Moray

Dragon Moray

M

MANATEE

Are mermaids really manatees? Christopher Columbus thought so. On one trip to the New World, members of his crew said they saw mermaids. Mermaids are supposed to have human heads and bodies and fish tails. Columbus later said that the creatures his crew saw were probably manatees. Manatees are mammals that usually live in salt water and don't really look very much like humans.

Most manatees live in the Atlantic Ocean or in some of the rivers of Brazil and western Africa. Some also live in the warm rivers of Florida and may even reach the Carolinas during the summer.

Like all mammals, manatees must breathe air. But if they are resting, they can stay under water for more than 15 minutes at a time.

Also like other mammals, manatee mothers nurse their young. But the youngster gets its fresh milk from a strange place: a nipple located under its mother's flipper.

A newborn manatee weighs as much as an 8-year-old child, about 55 pounds. A grown manatee may weigh as much as a small cow. Manatees can eat up to 100 pounds of plants in one day.

M

MUSK DEER

Even with its sharp tusks showing, a musk deer looks too gentle to be dangerous. But looks can be deceiving. If one deer enters another's territory, the two animals will fight fiercely. These deer don't have antlers; they fight with their tusks. The battle usually ends when one deer is cut badly. But if the males are fighting over a female, they may keep at it until one of them is killed.

Musk deer are hard to find. They live deep in the mountains and forests of Asia, their native land. People hunt the males for their musk. Musk is a smelly, jellylike substance the deer use to mark their territories. When it is fresh and damp, the musk smells terrible. But when it dries, it is like perfume. In fact, people use it to make perfume.

MANDRILL

Some people say the mandrill is the most colorful mammal in the world. It's easy to see why. A thick network of blood vessels just under this monkey's skin turns the animal's nose a brilliant red. When the animal is excited, the color gets even redder. Put this next to the bright blue skin on its cheeks and you have a colorful signal that's hard to miss.

A mandrill uses more than its color to show how it feels.

If it shakes its head, that means it wants to be groomed. If it snarls and bares its teeth, that means it's trying to be friendly. But if it yawns, watch out! The animal is angry.

Mandrills, which live in western Africa, are thought to be the heaviest of all monkeys. Many weigh more than 100 pounds. Each adult male may have as many as five or ten mates in a large family that includes ten or so youngsters.

M

MARABOU STORK

When feeding themselves, adult marabou storks of Africa act a lot like vultures. They gulp down the remains of dead animals. But when their youngsters are hungry, parent storks bring live prey back to their nests.

The large, wrinkled pouch hanging from the bird's neck still puzzles scientists. They have seen the bird inflate the pouch. And they know that it contains air sacs that are connected to the bird's left nostril. But so far they don't know what the pouch does.

MARKHOR

Long, curved horns make the markhor (MAR-core) one of the world's most unusual-looking goats. Wild herds of these animals roam the rugged mountains of central Asia.

Unlike deer, which grow new antlers every summer, markhors keep their horns year round. Male markhors use their horns to fight each other for females at mating time.

Both males and females have horns and beards. But the males' horns are longer and their beards are shaggier.

N

NAKED MOLE RAT

In East Africa, naked mole rats live out of sight in more ways than one. They spend their entire lives hidden in the tunnels they dig under the hot soil. They are also truly "out of sight" because they are blind. They don't need eyes to see in the blackness of their tunnels.

Mole rats' favorite food is grass, but they don't have to come above ground to get it. They eat the roots of the grass. Their long front teeth are shaped just right for nibbling on roots and bulbs. And when mole rats need a longer tunnel, they chew their way through the earth.

Mole rats live in colonies with a class system all their own. "Frequent workers" dig tunnels and find food. The "infrequent workers" do the same kind of work, just not as much of it. The "nonworkers," the largest rats in the colony, do almost no work at all.

N

NUDIBRANCHS

Nudibranchs (NOO-di-branks) are ocean-going slugs. They are relatives of the slugs that live in people's yards. These colorful sea creatures breathe through gills on the outside of their bodies, or right through their skin.

Most nudibranchs are only a few inches long. They often get their coloring from the food they eat. One nudibranch that feeds on sponges turns yellow when it eats a yellow sponge. If it eats an orange sponge, it turns orange.

Scientists think that picking up different colors this way helps nudibranchs hide from their enemies. When the nudibranchs stop to eat, they blend into the background and disappear. But the bright colors of some nudibranchs may also warn predators that these slugs taste bad and should be left alone.

Some nudibranchs not only take on the color of their prey, but also steal their weapons. By covering dangerous jellyfish and sea anemones with slime, nudibranchs can eat the poisonous animals, deadly stinging cells and all. The nudibranchs then store the stinging cells in the tips of their own bodies. When a fish attacks one of these nudibranchs, it gets stung.

N

NARWHAL

Unicorns, horses with single, long horns, are creatures of myth and legend. But the one-tusked whales called narwhals (NARR-walls) can truly be called "unicorns of the sea."

Hundreds of years ago, whalers hunted narwhals for their tusks. Some whalers said the tusks were unicorn horns with magic power and sold them for a lot of money.

Today we know that the horns are really oversized teeth. Narwhals have a single pair of teeth in their upper jaws. But in male narwhals, one tooth grows through the lip, forming the tusk. Some-

times both teeth grow out, creating a two-tusked narwhal.

Narwhals measure from 13 to 16 feet long—not including the tusks, which may add another 8 or 9 feet. Scientists think the males may use the tusks as weapons when they fight each other over female narwhals at mating time.

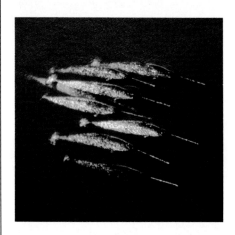

O

OCTOPUS

Octopuses are really shy. They like to squeeze into holes and under rocks, where they feel safe. These hiding places are also useful for ambushing crabs and other small animals octopuses like to eat. An

octopus's jaws are strong enough to bite through a lobster's thick shell. Sometimes an octopus will catch several creatures and store them in a web of skin that stretches between its arms. Octopuses may even eat each other, and old and sick ones have been seen nibbling on their own arms, which can grow back.

An octopus has three hearts. Two pump blood to the animal's gills to pick up oxygen. The third pushes the oxygen-rich blood back through the octopus's body.

When an octopus is attacked, it sends out a cloud of dark ink. The octopus takes off to safety behind this "smoke screen." It squeezes its body to force water out through a narrow funnel. The stream of water pushes the octopus forward, a natural form of jet propulsion.

O

ORANGUTAN

The orangutan is the "jungle man" of Borneo. That's what its name means in the native Malay language. The orangutan is the only ape that spends most of its life in trees. It is probably the heaviest tree-dweller in the world. A grown male may weigh over 200 pounds. As the males grow older, they develop large, fat cheek pouches.

OKAPI

Okapis look a lot like horses with stripes. In fact, when Europeans first saw these animals in 1900, they thought they were a type of horse. When scientists studied the skulls and teeth from okapis, they found out that okapis are short-necked cousins of giraffes. The okapis' large ears help them listen for danger in the dark African forests where they live. Their stripes help them blend in with the shadows and hide from their enemies.

P

PROBOSCIS MONKEY

What a nose! Male proboscis (pro-BAHSS-iss) monkeys of Borneo seem to be all snout. Why are their noses so big? People really don't know. Some scientists think that the monkeys use the noses as echo chambers to make their voices louder. The animals are said to sound like violins playing in the jungle. Other scientists say that female proboscis monkeys find large noses attractive. The larger a male's nose, the better chance he would have of getting a mate. Large noses can create problems for the monkeys, though. Sometimes males have to push them out of the way so they can eat.

P

PANGOLIN

This creature looks like a pine cone with legs. But it's really a pangolin making its way through the trees.

Pangolins live in Africa and India. When they climb trees, they wrap their strong tails around branches to hold on. On the ground, they use their tails as braces when they walk on their hind legs.

Overlapping scales protect pangolins from enemies small and large. Each scale is like a thick fingernail with a sharp edge. With a quick flick of its scales, a pangolin can knock tiny pests off its back. And when threatened by a large enemy, a pangolin curls up into a ball (above left).

A good sense of smell helps pangolins find food. They usually eat ants and termites. First a pangolin rips into the insects' nest with its sharp claws. Then it pokes in its long, sticky tongue and pulls out a mouthful of insects. Pangolins don't chew their food because they don't have teeth. But small pebbles in their stomachs help pangolins mash the swallowed insects.

A person poking into an ant or termite nest would be bitten. But these insects can't bother a pangolin. Scales, thick eyelids, and flaps that cover its nose and ears keep a pangolin from feeling bites.

P

PEACOCK FLOUNDER

It's easy to see what's odd about the peacock flounder. Both its eyes are on the same side of its head. When a peacock flounder hatches, it looks normal. It swims upright, with one eye on the right side of its body and the other eye on the left side. But soon the right eye starts moving over toward the left side. The change takes three or four months to complete. By the time both eyes are on the left side, the flounder has started swimming on its side, with its eyes facing up. Some other flounders end up with both eyes on the right side of their bodies.

PLATYPUS

Platypuses are fakes! That is what people said when they first saw a skin from one of these Australian mammals. The skin was furry like a mammal, but the head had a bill that looked like a duck's bill.

Today, we know that platypuses really are mammals. They use their rubbery bills to poke into riverbeds for food. They also have poison spurs—small, hollow horns—on each of their hind feet. And, strangest of all, they lay eggs. When the young platypuses hatch, their mothers nurse them in their grass-lined nests for up to four months.

QUETZAL

Are quetzals (KET-sulls) the prettiest birds in the world? The Aztec Indians of Mexico used to think so. Only Aztec noblemen were allowed to wear clothes decorated with the birds' long, green feathers. Today, the people of Guatemala still honor the birds by putting their pictures on the nation's stamps and money.

Male quetzals are prettier than female quetzals. Their bright tail feathers stretch nearly two feet behind them. The long feathers create problems for the birds when they try to fly. The birds can't take off from a tree the way other birds do because the tail feathers drag across the branches. So, the birds jump off limbs backwards.

The long tails also get in the way when the males sit on eggs in their nests. The birds' nests are holes in trees. People used to think the birds needed two holes for their nests. The males would enter through one hole, sit on the eggs, then go straight out through the other hole. That way, the long tail wouldn't get bent or broken. We now know that one hole is enough. The birds can turn around and leave the way they went in. But even then the nesting males often leave the tips of their tails sticking out the entrance.

Manta Ray

Electric Ray

Stingray

Eagle Ray

R

RAYS

They look like flying wings, soaring through the oceans. But they are rays—strange, flat fish that are relatives of the sharks. Like sharks, rays don't have scales. And instead of bones, they have skeletons made of cartilage (like the tip of your nose).

Manta rays (left) are the largest of all the rays. The biggest one ever measured stretched 60 feet across and weighed over 5,000 pounds. Unlike most rays, which live and eat near the ocean floor, mantas swim near the surface.

Electric rays (bottom left) are aggressive hunters. First, they wrap their winglike fins around other fish. Then they zap their prey with up to 220 volts of electricity. With their prey too stunned to get away, the electric rays can easily finish off their meals.

More people are hurt by *stingrays* (bottom center) than by any other fish. These rays hide on the ocean floor, covered with sand. When someone steps on a stingray, the ray usually strikes at him with its tail, which has poisonous barbs.

Eagle rays (bottom right) are graceful swimmers. They measure about seven feet across and eat a wide variety of food, from crabs and lobsters to small fish.

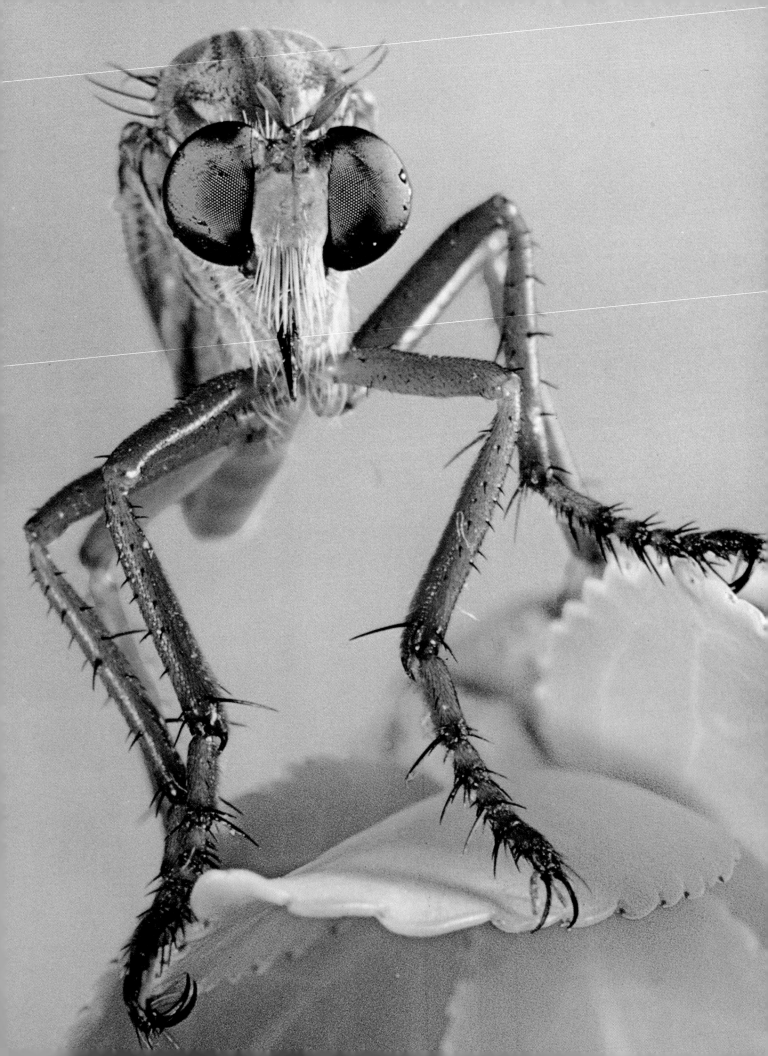

R

ROBBER FLY

The robber fly acts like an insect gangster. It chases almost any insect that moves. It grabs its victim with its strong, bristly legs. Then the robber fly stabs it with its sharp snout and sucks out its insides, leaving an empty skin.

Some robber flies are the largest flies in the world. They measure up to three inches long. They are strong enough to capture bees, wasps, and large grasshoppers.

Robber fly larvae may spend up to three years underground, eating worms and grubs. But once they mature, the adult robber flies live for barely a month.

REMORA

The remora (REM-or-ah) is the hitchhiker of the sea. This fish swims up to a shark or other large fish and presses the flat disk on top of its head against the host fish's body. The disk works like a suction cup and holds the two fish together. That way the remora gets a free ride. Besides getting a lift, the remora may get to feed on scraps left over from the host's meals. Some people say that the remora returns the favor by picking parasites off its host.

Fishermen from Africa to Japan sometimes use remoras as living fishhooks. They tie a line to a remora's tail and let the remora stick itself onto a turtle or fish. Then they pull in the remora and its catch.

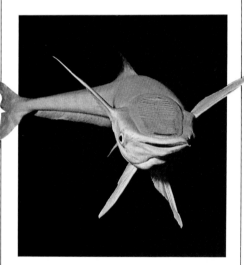

S

SUN SPIDER

If any animal deserves the nickname "jaws," it's the sun spider. This two-inch-long creature will attack almost any small animal. It even chews up lizards many times its own size. It chomps its victims into soft pieces and sucks up the juices. Sucking up the juices is important because the sun spider must get all its liquids this way. It never drinks water.

Though the sun spider looks like a spider, it isn't one. It is a close relative of both scorpions and spiders. It was named the "sun" spider because it lives where the climate is sunny and hot.

S

SLOTH

Try hanging upside down from a tree for awhile. Tiring, isn't it? But sloths, which live in South and Central America, spend most of their time doing just that. They even sleep hanging from a branch. They can hang on so well because three curved claws on each foot hook around branches. The hooks work so well that when a sloth dies, it often remains hanging from the tree.

A baby sloth uses its claws to hold onto its mother's fur. When it matures, it will also swing hand over hand through the trees, munching leaves.

Sloths aren't in any hurry to get anywhere. They sleep about 18 hours a day. When a sloth does get going, it moves about one mile per hour. Sloths are the slowest land mammals in the world.

A sloth's thick hairs have thin grooves. Tiny plants called algae grow in the grooves. When it rains, the algae turn very green, and the sloth looks like a moss-covered branch.

These slow movements and green hair seem strange to us. But they help sloths survive. Because sloths look like part of a tree, their main enemies—jaguars and eagles—have a hard time seeing them.

S

SPIRAL GILL WORM

Who would have thought that worms could be pretty? They can be. Spiral gill worms add bright colors to the reefs in the Coral Sea near Australia where they live. This picture shows several of the worms' colorful spiral gills, pushed out to get oxygen and food from the water. The rest of the worms' bodies are long and narrow. They stay in hard tubes stuck in the coral.

Since these worms can't crawl away, they look like easy prey for hungry fish to catch. But if even a shadow touches the feeding worms, they pull their gills back into their hard tubes and wait until the danger has passed.

SCALLOP

What common sea creatures see through more than 100 blue eyes but have no faces, strain their food but have no teeth, and swim quickly but have no fins? The answer: scallops (top, right).

A scallop's eyes look like tiny blue dots lining the edges of its shell. It can't see very well, though. Its eyes can only detect the difference between light and dark. A shadow crossing it could mean an enemy is approaching.

If an eye breaks off, a scallop grows another. A scallop can replace all its eyes in just a few weeks.

Scallops usually rest on the ocean floor, feeding. As water flows over their gills, special filters on the gills strain out tiny bits of food. But if an octopus or starfish comes by, they're off in a flash. Scallops don't even have to see the creatures' shadows. They can smell the animals coming in time to get away.

To swim away, a scallop snaps its shell shut. The closing shell squirts water out of small openings and pushes the scallop forward.

SEA SPIDER

"All legs and no body" is a good way to describe the sea spider (bottom, right). All this little animal's organs are inside its legs. When it eats, the food goes right into the legs where it is absorbed by special cells. These cells then break loose and pass the food around to the other cells.

Normally, the male uses two of its legs to clean itself. But when there are fertilized eggs to take care of, it uses these legs to carry the eggs around. Once the young sea spiders hatch, they float off to latch onto other animals until they grow their own legs.

Like beetles, crabs, and centipedes, sea spiders are distant relatives of the real spiders. Most adult sea spiders are small. The one shown here is barely an inch across. But in really cold seas, some sea spiders grow legs a foot long.

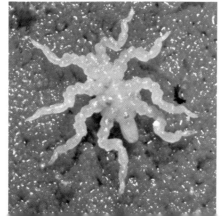

Rainbow Snake

Cobra and Mongoose

Sea Snake

S

SNAKES

Who said snakes are scary? Once you get to know about snakes, these reptiles are among the most fascinating animals on earth.

Have you ever tried to run in soft, hot sand? It's not easy. But the *sidewinder* (far left) has no problem crossing the scorching deserts in the southwestern United States where it lives. The snake moves sideways, letting just two parts of its body touch the sand at one time.

Many snakes can swim as well as they can crawl. Poisonous *sea snakes* (bottom) spend most of their lives under water in tropical oceans. While in the water, they use their poisonous bite to paralyze the eels and small fish they eat.

An Asian *cobra* (center) can kill an elephant with one bite on the soft tip of the elephant's trunk. But the snake has a hard time when it attacks a little mongoose. The mongoose jumps around the snake and bites it in the head.

According to folk stories, the *rainbow snake* (top) of the southeastern United States rolls downhill like a hoop and stings prey with its pointed tail. In reality, this non-poisonous snake prefers swimming after eels. And the sharp tip of its tail is harmless.

S

SCIMITAR BABBLER

In this photograph, the scimitar (SIM-ih-tar) babbler looks like a "nosy" but quiet bird. But in real life, this Asian forest dweller joins other babblers in nearly constant chatter. Even though these restless birds often can't be seen, their loud, babbling noise almost always gives them away. In fact, the name *babbler* means "foolish talker."

The bird's beak, shaped like the curved sword called a scimitar, looks too awkward to be useful. But the babbler finds it just right for picking up ants and other insects.

STAR-NOSED MOLE

North America's star-nosed mole lives to dig and digs to live. Day and night, all year round, it burrows through damp soil searching for grubs and earthworms to eat. This mole is a good swimmer and diver, too. It catches fish and pokes around river bottoms for other water creatures.

Scientists believe that the mole uses its star-shaped nose to help it find food. As the mole walks through its tunnels or swims in the water, it keeps most of its nose's 22 fleshy rays in constant motion, feeling for something to eat.

STAG BEETLE

This male stag beetle looks dangerous with its long "antlers"—which are really its jaws. But its jaws are not strong enough to bite very hard. Stag beetles with short jaws can pinch much harder.

When male insects fight over females, the strongest ones usually win. Over the years, many types of stag beetle have developed short, strong jaws that help them fight. But other types of stag beetle continue to grow large jaws, even though their jaws seem to get in the way. These beetles can't fight very well with their large jaws. And they don't seem to use them to get food. The truth is, no one knows what the super jaws are good for.

TOUCAN

Some toucans have bills as long as the rest of their bodies. It's a wonder that the birds can hold their heads up. But toucans have a secret. The walls of the bill are thin, but strong. And the space between the walls is filled with air and light fibers.

Besides picking fruit and seeds to eat, toucans have fun with their bills. In a game like "King of the Mountain," one toucan tries to push another one off its branch by poking at it with its bill. And one toucan may use its bill to toss berries for another toucan to catch.

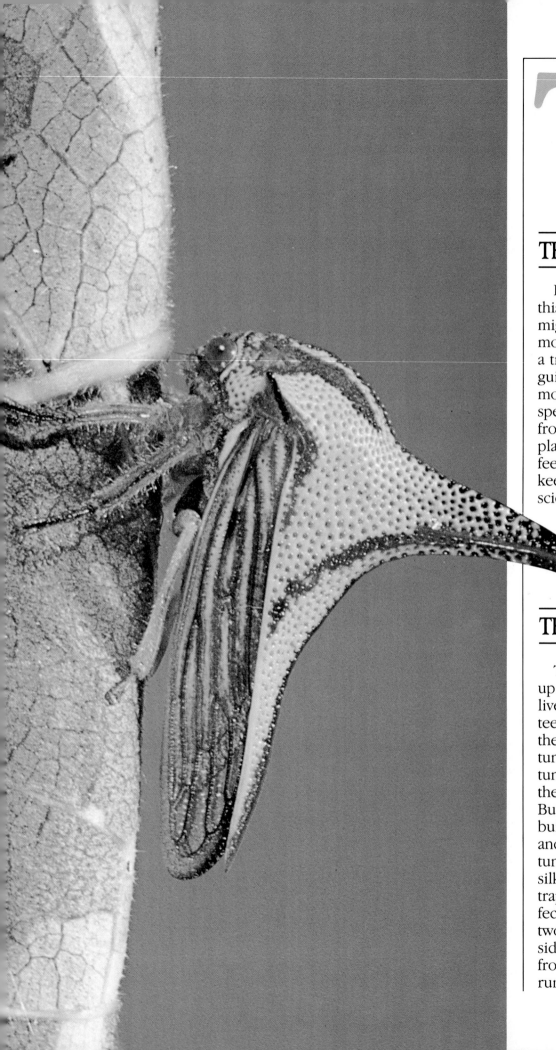

T

TREEHOPPER

If you took a close look at this thorn on a plant, you might be surprised to see it move. It isn't a thorn at all. It's a treehopper in a clever disguise. Treehoppers, usually no more than a half-inch long, spend their days sucking juices from fruit trees and other plants. The disguise hides the feeding insects from their keen-eyed enemies. Some scientists also think that the thorny shape makes treehoppers so hard to eat that other creatures just don't try.

TRAPDOOR SPIDER

The trapdoor spider lives up to its name. It really does live under a trapdoor. Using its teeth and fangs, this critter—the size of a quarter—digs a tunnel up to a foot long. The tunnel, just wide enough for the spider, is lined with silk. But that's not all. The spider builds a trapdoor out of soil and silk and attaches it to the tunnel opening with a hinge of silk. Like a manhole cover, the trapdoor fits the tunnel perfectly. The spider also makes two small holes in the underside of the lid. To get away from its enemies, the spider runs into its tunnel, reaches into the holes with two of its eight legs, and holds the trapdoor shut.

The trapdoor is built to protect the spider from its main enemy, the hunting wasp, but it is useful in other ways. It keeps out dust and debris and rain. And it helps the spider snag meals. As shown here, the trapdoor spider hides beneath its lid and pounces on insects that come too close.

THORNY DEVIL

Most animals drink with their mouths. So does Australia's thorny devil. But it also collects water with its entire body. When the animal touches anything that is wet, tiny grooves between its scales fill with water. And on cool, damp nights, the grooves fill up with dew. When the thorny devil opens its mouth, the water flows through the grooves and into its mouth.

The spiny hump on the thorny devil's back puzzles biologists. Some say that when there is nothing to drink, the lizard turns some of the fat into water. Others think that when the lizard is in danger, it pushes up the hump to look like another head and draw attention from its real head. So far, the thorny devil's hump remains a real mystery.

T

TARSIER

Furry little tarsiers (TAR-see-urs) have huge eyes built for seeing into the dark forest at night. That's when they hunt for insects, lizards, and small birds to eat.

Even when they rest, tarsiers sit with one eye open. That way they can keep track of their enemies. Tarsiers' eyes each measure just a half-inch across. But they seem to fill up half the animals' heads. If our eyes took up as much space in *our* heads as a tarsier's eyes take up in *its* head, they would be bigger than tennis balls.

Tarsiers are in a family by themselves. Although they look like monkeys, they are only distant relatives.

U

UAKARI

It's easy to think that uakaris (wah-KAR-ees) are angry or embarrassed because angry or embarrassed people often get red faces. But the faces of these South American monkeys are always red, though some uakaris turn pale if they stay out of the sun.

Uakaris live in the jungle treetops around the Amazon River. They travel in groups of a dozen or more in search of fruit, their favorite food. Every now and then, they eat a tasty leaf or insect.

Usually, uakaris are quiet. But when uakaris try to figure out who's boss, watch out! They start fighting and making a lot of noise. Most of the time, however, there is more noise than fight. The fighters seldom hurt each other.

Scientists are worried about uakaris. The monkeys normally live far away from towns and villages. But as people clear more jungle to make homes, the uakaris may someday have no place to live.

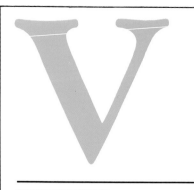

VIPERFISH

The viperfish lives far down in the ocean where there is no light. But darkness is no problem for this 10-inch-long creature. It carries its own lighting system. Hundreds of glowing spots line the roof of its mouth. A double row of lights runs the length of its body on both sides. And a long spine on its back ends in a tip that also glows. When curious fish come near, attracted by the light, the viperfish snags them for its dinner.

The viperfish stabs its prey with teeth as sharp as needles. Moveable teeth in its throat force the prey into its stomach. Sometimes these fish swallow prey much bigger than themselves. Muscles open the viperfish's jaws extra wide and force its heart and gills out of the way to make room for the large meal.

VELVET ANT

Velvet ants are not ants at all. They are wasps with long stingers that can kill other insects. The wingless females are covered with a layer of hair as soft as velvet. That's why these insects got their name.

Beneath their furry coat, velvet ants have a thick shell that acts like armor. It's a good thing, too. These wasps lay their eggs in the nests of other wasps and bees. When the eggs hatch, the velvet ant larvae eat the food that the other insects have stored for their own young. Sometimes the velvet ant larvae eat those other young insects, too. So wasps and bees don't want velvet ants near their homes. They try to drive the unwanted visitors away by stinging them. The velvet ants need their armor and sharp stingers to protect themselves.

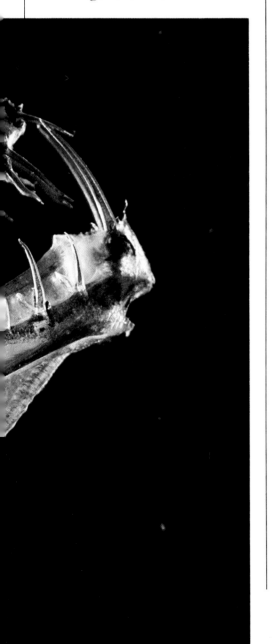

WARTHOG

Warthogs are downright ugly. Their faces are covered with warts and bristly hair. And funny-looking tusks stick out sideways from their jaws. But to other animals in the wild, warthogs are lean, mean, fighting machines.

These 200-pound animals are not aggressive, but they fight fearlessly if threatened. They can inflict severe wounds with their tusks. One female warthog protecting her young actually charged an elephant that was chasing her.

Warthogs prefer to eat tender grass tips. But when grass is scarce, they pick berries and dig for roots. Because their necks are short, warthogs often kneel down on their front legs to eat.

WANDERING LEAF

Hiding in plain sight is easy for the wandering leaf insect of Asia. When it spreads out on a leaf—presto!—it disappears. The insect's wide body and flat, green legs match the color and shape of the leaves in the jungles where it lives. That disguise makes it hard for a predator to see the insect. If a predator does attack a young wandering leaf and happens to grab its leg, this insect breaks

it off to get away. Later it grows another one.

The wandering leaf belongs to a family of some 2,000 insects that all look like leaves or sticks. When some of these insects are ready to have youngsters, the females just lay eggs. They don't have to mate as most animals do. Some groups have no males at all.

WALKING CATFISH

Like most catfish, walking catfish spend a lot of time near the bottoms of lakes and streams. There they use their eight sensitive whiskers, called barbels, to find mussels, worms, fish, and plants to eat. But when the food supply runs

out, walking catfish do something no other catfish can do. They climb out of the water and walk off to find food somewhere else.

Walking catfish don't have legs. But they do have a stiff spine in each of their two front fins. They jab one spine into the ground, push ahead with their bodies, then jab in the other spine. They can zig and zag like this for more than a quarter of a mile.

Most fish die soon after being removed from water. But walking catfish can live in air for several hours. Special organs behind their gills work like lungs and permit the catfish to breathe air.

WEEVILS

Weevils nibbling on plants can be destructive. But up close, some of these insects are also colorful and fascinating. There are more than 50,000 kinds of weevils. That makes weevils the largest animal family in the world.

The *acorn weevil* (large photo) looks funny with its curved snout. The two antennae sticking out to the side help the weevil smell. The female weevil uses jaws on her snout to chew into acorns. The egg she lays in each acorn will hatch into a grub and eat the inside of the acorn.

Like all weevils, the *polka-dot weevils* (top left) have hard shells. The shells protect the weevils' insides. Most weevils have dull, plain colors. But these bright creatures look hand painted.

South America's *bird-dropping weevil* (top center) looks dead. But that's the whole idea. A hungry predator would probably ignore the weevil, thinking it was just a bird dropping.

Like the bird-dropping weevil, the *giraffe weevil* (top right) of Madagascar also plays dead. The weevil's long neck, which is really part of its stretched-out skull, still puzzles scientists. They have no idea why the weevil has such a strange shape.

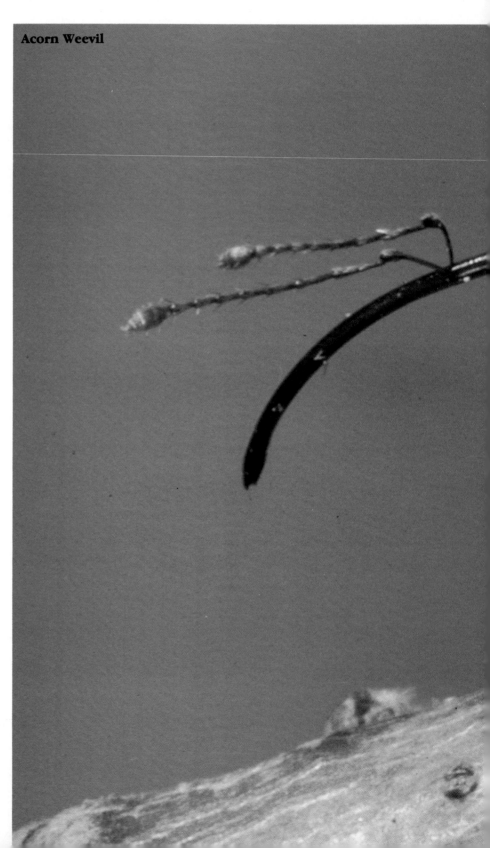

Acorn Weevil

Polka-dot Weevils

Bird-dropping Weevil

Giraffe Weevil

X-RAY FISH

Imagine fish that show off their insides. X-ray fish do that all the time—because their skin is almost as clear as glass.

Sometimes these fish don't look transparent in pictures. That's because reflections from the photographer's flash make the fish look shiny instead of clear. But in an aquarium, you can see the fish's skeletons.

X-ray fish are only about two inches long. Their native home is South America, where they live in warm rivers. Their sharp teeth are used to eat insect larvae and small worms. X-ray fish are closely related to more dangerous sharp-toothed fish, the piranhas.

One problem with keeping X-ray fish in a home aquarium is their appetite for meat. You have to make sure they don't eat their own young.

YUCCA MOTH

If all the yucca moths in America were to die, there would soon be no yucca plants. Or if something happened to the yucca plants, the moths would disappear too. These insects and plants are partners. They depend on each other for survival.

In the spring, female yucca moths fly from one yucca plant to another. They lay their eggs inside the plants' large, white flowers. At the same time, the moths carry pollen between the plants. After laying her eggs, a female sticks the pollen into the plants' seed organs. The pollen fertilizes the seeds so they will grow.

When the young moths start to grow inside the plant, they feed on some of the seeds. But without moths to carry the pollen, the plants' seeds would not develop at all. No more plants would grow. And without the yucca seeds to eat, the moth larvae would starve.

YAK

Yaks are a kind of long-haired cattle that live in Asia. Once wild, yaks are now mostly domesticated. People have been raising yaks for nearly 3,000 years. Many people throughout Central Asia

depend on these cattle for milk, fur, and meat. Today, the few yaks that remain in the wild live in parts of northern Tibet and China.

Yaks' long fur keeps them warm when winter winds blow and the temperature is 40 degrees below zero. Though yaks look awkward, they are good climbers. In the summer, yak herds head far up into the mountains. They graze at higher altitudes than any other large mammals in the world.

Z

ZEBRA LOOKALIKES

With their bold black-and-white stripes, *zebras* (right, above) look as though they would stand out in a crowd. Actually, their stripes help them hide. If zebras stand in tall grass, their stripes blend into the shadows made by the grass. And when zebras stand in a group, it is hard for a predator to tell where one zebra ends and another one begins. That probably makes it confusing for the predator to figure out just where to strike.

Zebras aren't alone. Many animals have zebralike stripes. Sometimes the stripes hide the animals from their enemies. Sometimes the stripes call attention to the creatures that have them.

The horizontal black-and-white stripes on their tails gave male *zebra finches* (below, left) their names. The patterns and colors of these Australian birds help the birds attract mates.

Zebra

Zebra Finch

Zebra Angelfish

Bright patterns seem to help *zebra angelfish* (below, center) get noticed, too. But the stripes don't appear to attract mates. They probably warn other angelfish to stay out of this fish's territory.

Like the zebras, the *zebra butterflies* (below, right) find their stripes a helpful disguise. Zebra butterflies are easy to spot in open sunlight. But in the dark parts of their dense jungle homes, they are hard to see. Their stripes look like shadows on leaves.

A common question is, "Are these animals black with white stripes or white with black stripes?" Not much has been written about the stripes of the finch, the angelfish, or the butterfly. But a scientist studying zebras found one whose stripes had not developed completely. He saw that the incomplete stripes were just a few spots of white—and that without its stripes, the zebra was black.

Zebra Butterfly

ILLUSTRATION CREDITS

Cover: Zig Leszczynski/Animals Animals. **Page 1:** James H. Carmichael, Jr. **2-3:** Michael Fogden/OSF/Animals Animals. **4-5:** F. Gohier/National Audubon Society Collection/PR. **5:** Top, Tom McHugh/National Audubon Society Collection/PR; bottom left: Marilyn K. Krog; bottom right, Stan Wayman. **6:** F. G. Irwin. **7:** Top, Sharon Kurgis; bottom, Jane Burton/Bruce Coleman, Inc. **8-9:** Peter David/Seaphot. **10:** Left, Tui De Roy; right, Dr. Thomas Eisner and Dr. Daniel Aneshansley. **10-11:** Kjell B. Sandved. **12-13:** J. Scott Altenbach and Merlin D. Tuttle/Bat Conservation International/Milwaukee Public Museum. **13:** Top, Kenneth Fink/National Audubon Society Collection/PR; middle and bottom, Merlin D. Tuttle/Bat Conservation International/Milwaukee Public Museum. **14:** Keith Gillet/Tom Stack & Assoc. **14-15:** J. B. Davidson/Survival Anglia/Oxford Scientific Films. **16:** Top, Barry Mansell; bottom, Kjell B. Sandved. **17:** C. B. Frith/Bruce Coleman, Ltd. **18:** left, Carl W. Rettenmeyer; right, Graham Pizzey. **19:** All, John MacGregor. **20-21:** Alex Kerstitch. **22:** Top and bottom, Tom McHugh/National Audubon Society Collection/PR. **23:** David Cavagnaro. **24:** Jeff Foott. **25:** Top, G. E. Schmida/Bruce Coleman, Inc.; bottom, Grant Haist. **26:** Christian Petron/Seaphot. **26-27:** Kenneth Lucas. **28:** E. R. Degginger. **29:** Top left, George H. Harrison; bottom left, M. Philip Kahl; top right, E. R. Degginger;

middle right, Zig Leszczynski/Animals Animals; bottom right, Alan Blank/Bruce Coleman, Inc. **30-31:** Fred Bavendam. **32:** Edward S. Ross. **32-33:** E. R. Degginger. **33:** John Conway. **34-35:** Tom McHugh/National Audubon Society Collection/PR. **36:** Howard Hall. **37:** Aldo Margiocco. **38:** Top, Rod Planck/Tom Stack & Assoc.; bottom, Tui De Roy. **39:** Top, Ron Austing; bottom, Philip Sayers/Seaphot. **40-41:** Peter Parks/Oxford Scientific Films. **41:** Top and bottom, Douglas Faulkner/Sally Faulkner Collection; second from top, Keith Gillet; third from top, E. R. Degginger. **42:** Wayne Lynch. **43:** Michael Fogden/Animals Animals. **44:** Tom McHugh/National Audubon Society Collection/PR. **45:** R. Kuiter/IKAN. **46:** Jeff Lepore. **47:** Left, Chris Newbert; right, Steve Martin/Tom Stack & Assoc. **48:** Top, Jeff Rotman; middle and bottom, Carl Roessler. **49:** E. R. Degginger. **50-51:** Jeff Foott. **52:** Stanley Breeden. **53:** George H. Harrison/Grant Heilman Photography. **54:** M. Philip Kahl. **55:** Left, Collection Varin Visage/Jacana; right, Jen & Des Bartlett/Bruce Coleman, Inc. **56:** Left and right, Anthony Bannister. **56-57:** Alex Kerstitch. **57:** Left, Gordon A. Robilliard; middle, Anthony Bannister; right, Jeff Foott. **58:** Top, Fred Bruemmer; bottom, K. J. Finley. **58-59:** Ed Robinson/Tom Stack & Assoc. **60:** Tom McHugh/National Audubon Society Collection/PR. **61:** Left, George Holton/National Audubon Society Collection/PR; right, Miriam Austerman/Animals Animals. **62-63:** Keith & Liz Laidler/Ardea. **63:** Mandal Ranjit/National Audubon Society Collection/PR. **64:** Top, Carl Roessler; bottom, Graham

Pizzey. **65:** Michael Fogden/Oxford Scientific Films. **66:** Left, Howard Hall; right, Alex Double/Seaphot. **66-67:** Carl Roessler. **67:** Ed Robinson/Tom Stack & Assoc. **68:** Grace A. Thompson. **69:** Top, Douglas Faulkner/Sally Faulkner Collection; bottom, David Hughes/Bruce Coleman, Ltd. **70-71:** Carl W. Rettenmeyer. **72-73:** Howard Hall. **73:** Top, Jack Dermid; bottom, Jeff Foott. **74-75:** M. P. L. Fogden/Bruce Coleman, Inc. **75:** Top, Jack Dermid; middle, Norman Myers/Bruce Coleman, Inc.; bottom, Carl Roessler. **76:** Top, Constance P. Warner; bottom, Rod Planck/Tom Stack & Assoc. **77:** Betty Randall. **78-79:** Keith & Liz Laidler/Ardea. **80:** Kjell B. Sandved. **81:** Top, A. Cosmos Blank/National Audubon Society Collection/PR; bottom, Hans & Judy Beste/Tom Stack & Assoc. **82:** Anthony Mercieca. **83:** Christian Zuber/Bruce Coleman, Ltd. **84-85:** Peter Parks/Oxford Scientific Films. **85:** James H. Robinson. **86:** Leonard Lee Rue III. **87:** Top, E. R. Degginger; bottom, Tom Myers. **88-89:** Edward S. Ross. **89:** Left, Kjell B. Sandved; middle and right, Edward S. Ross. **90:** Hans Reinhard/Bruce Coleman, Ltd. **91:** Top, Robert P. Carr/Bruce Coleman, Ltd.; bottom, Mark N. Boulton/Bruce Coleman, Inc. **92:** Hans & Judy Beste/Ardea. **92-93:** Top, Norman Myers/Bruce Coleman, Inc.; bottom, Douglas Faulkner/Sally Faulkner Collection. **93:** K. G. Preston-Mafham/Animals Animals. **95:** E. R. Degginger. **96:** Tui De Roy.

INDEX

Illustrations appear in *italics*.

Library of Congress Cataloging-in-Publication Data

Main entry under title:

Incredible animals A to Z.

  Includes index.
  Summary: A photographic survey, done in alphabetical order, of some of the world's most unusual animals, inhabitants of the land, sea, and air, with descriptions of their physical characteristics and behavior.
  l. Animals—Dictionaries, Juvenile.
[l. Animals—Dictionaries] I. National Wildlife Federation. II. Ranger Rick.

QL9.I53 1985   591'.03'21   85-15260

ISBN 0-912186-66-6

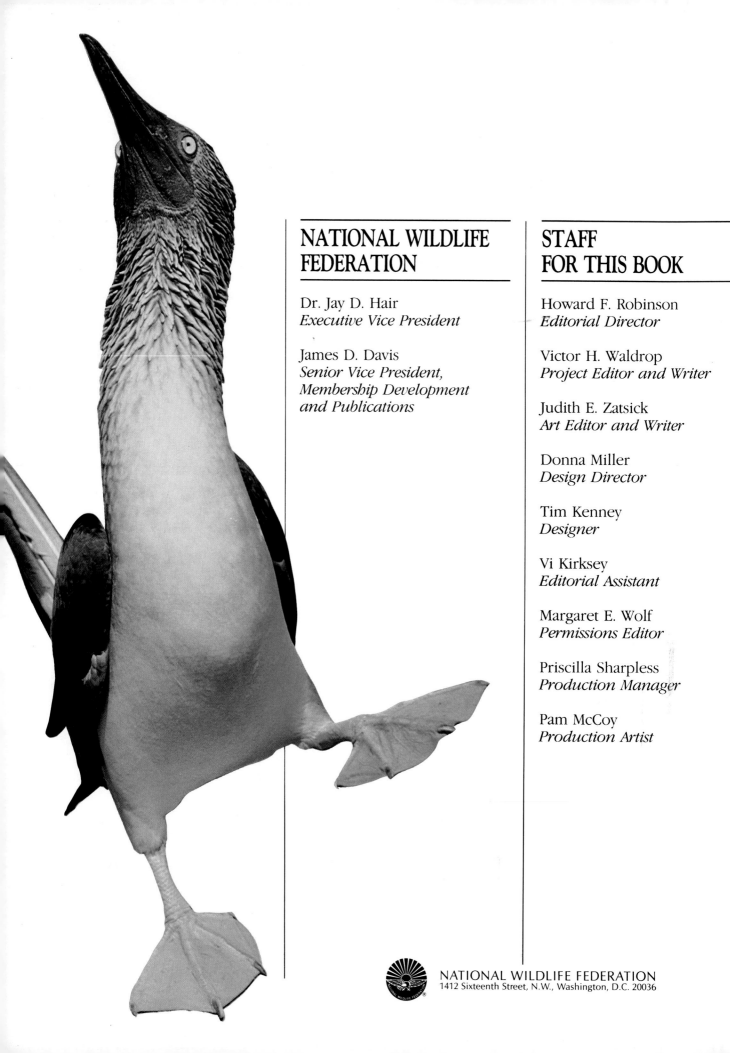

NATIONAL WILDLIFE FEDERATION

Dr. Jay D. Hair
Executive Vice President

James D. Davis
Senior Vice President,
Membership Development
and Publications

STAFF FOR THIS BOOK

Howard F. Robinson
Editorial Director

Victor H. Waldrop
Project Editor and Writer

Judith E. Zatsick
Art Editor and Writer

Donna Miller
Design Director

Tim Kenney
Designer

Vi Kirksey
Editorial Assistant

Margaret E. Wolf
Permissions Editor

Priscilla Sharpless
Production Manager

Pam McCoy
Production Artist

NATIONAL WILDLIFE FEDERATION
1412 Sixteenth Street, N.W., Washington, D.C. 20036